Light
to live by

an exploration in
Quaker spirituality

The English version of the Cary Lecture 2001

Rex Ambler

A companion volume to
Truth of the Heart, also from Quaker Books

This Richard Cary Lecture was first published in
German under the title *Licht, darin zu Leben*
© 2001 Religiöse Geschellschaft der Freunde
(Quaker) Deutsche Jahresversammlung

First published by Quaker Books in 2002
This edition published in 2008 by Quaker Books,
Friends House, 173 Euston Road, London NW1 2BJ

www.quaker.org.uk

ISBN 978 0 85245 336 0

Printed by Information Press Ltd

CONTENTS

ACKNOWLEDGEMENTS

To Kristen Richardson who typed up the first draft;
and to Ian Breckenridge, Susan Glover Frykman,
Christopher Holdsworth and other members of the ·
Literature Committee of Britain Yearly Meeting who
helped with the revision for the English edition.
Hugh Barbour has kindly given permission to quote
from his *Early Quaker Writings*.

ABBREVIATIONS

OT   Original text

TME   Translation into Modern English

TOTH   *Truth of the Heart: an anthology of George Fox*,
        edited by Rex Ambler, Quaker Books, 2001.

Works *Works of George Fox*, 8 volumes, 1831,
        reprinted by the George Fox Fund,
        State College, Pennsylvania, 1990.

My lecture will be quite personal, in two respects. It will describe a personal practice of meditation which I discovered in early Friends, and it will tell the story of that discovery and of my attempts to use the practice and develop it in my own personal life. Even so I am surprised, on reading what I have written, that it is so much about me! This was not my intention. I had wanted to tell you of this Quaker practice in quite objective terms, without interference from my own feelings and opinions about it. But the fact is that in order to understand this practice and what its possibilities are I had to try it out for myself. And in this Quaker form of meditation, as you will see, that is where you have to begin, with yourself and your own situation. So I had no alternative but to make myself the object of my own experiment. When I was confident enough to share my experiences, others could join me in the experiment and try out the meditation for themselves. We could then share what we had discovered and learn from one another. But that is later in the story. The first part has to be autobiographical.

1. Searching

Seven years ago I had two things on my mind that I could not resolve. One was an intellectual problem about what the early Quakers were saying they had experienced. The other was a spiritual problem about how to resolve an anxiety of my own. They had little to do with each other, or so it seemed at the time. Only when I began to see a resolution to them could I also see how closely they were connected.

The intellectual problem is one you may be familiar with yourselves. The first Quakers, of the middle seventeenth century, had obviously made a great discovery. It not only changed their lives, giving them peace of mind and great joy, but it also fired them up to share what they had found and to hold to it even when they were imprisoned and beaten for doing so. But what had they discovered? Their descriptions are simple and poetic, but still difficult to understand. They talked of 'the light' within them that showed them the way, 'the truth' that set them free, 'the life' which sprang up within them and between them, and 'the power' which enabled them to do the seemingly impossible. What were they talking about? What meaning did these simple but elusive words have for them?

I had a research student at the time writing a doctoral dissertation on the development of early Quakerism. She was equally puzzled by the meaning of that early Quaker language, and remained so, even though she came to write an excellent dissertation on the history of their movement.[1] As a mature student she was already an expert on the period, which I was not, so I had hoped she would find some answers. I kept asking her as she ploughed through the literature of that time, 'But what did they mean by "the light", "the spirit", "the covenant of life" and so on?' 'You're the theologian,' she would reply, 'you tell me.' She was right, of course, so I decided it was time I found out for myself.

Meanwhile I still had a spiritual worry. There was an anxiety that had dogged me for many years and had now caught up with me as I found myself in difficulty in two relationships that were important to me. I was not being entirely honest with these people. I was pretending that I was quite happy with them and with the way things were between us, despite the fact that we occasionally had fearful rows or misunderstandings. I had got as far as understanding that hiding my true feelings, though intended to make things better, was in fact making them far worse. I had gained the understanding partly through psychotherapy, which I had undertaken at various times of crisis in my life, and which I always found wholesome and beneficial. But I was now asking myself why I shouldn't be able to resolve this new crisis myself. After all I was a Quaker. I believed I had 'that of God' in me which could give me insight and strength and a capacity to love. But the fact was, as I had to admit to myself, I did not know how to access it. Nor did I know any other Quaker who would be able to help me do this. There were Friends who could give me advice and there was the Meeting of Friends for worship when some resolution might be expected to come. But though I had often been inspired by Meeting I had never known an experience of such depth that it challenged the basic issues of my life or fundamentally changed me. And 'advice' was not what I was looking for. Was my Quaker faith then unable to help me in a time of personal crisis? Did it after all have no depth, or power or practical effectiveness? These questions haunted me as I struggled as best I could with two unhappy relationships, and continued to do so for many months.

I made better progress with my studies. I started by reading Hugh Barbour's *The Quakers in Puritan England*, which gave me important clues as to how to understand their experience and therefore the language they used to describe it. I had already gone through the large collection

of *Early Quaker Writings* he had compiled with Arthur
Roberts,[2] where they briefly explained the Quaker experience, and I should have picked up my clues from that, but
I had read the book twenty years before and I hadn't then
acquired the experience that would enable me to recognise
its significance. Nevertheless it sowed a seed, and reading it
again now I can see why I came to suspect that early
Quakers still had a lot to teach us. In the 'Introduction',
Barbour and Roberts wrote this – I had marked it in pencil.

> The Light, a metaphor which suggests a searchlight
> into a well or a candle in a dark closet and not man's
> own mental power, is not to be distinguished in early
> Quaker experience from Christ or the Spirit within
> men. The Light searched out sin and brought into
> sight all of a man's inward emotions and outward
> acts, showing a man who he was, as through long
> evenings alone or at Quaker gatherings the hearer
> opened himself to Christ's Spirit for redemption. In
> the silence, *every* act and motive was branded as the
> fruit of self-will…in the little groups or Meetings
> those who had gone through the experience could
> help those still wrestling with the deeper discoveries
> of self-deception….
>
> In the journals we find Friends describing how
> the same Light that revealed all self-willed acts and
> motives as evil, began after a period of waiting and
> openness to prompt positive acts just as specifically.[3]

What obviously impressed me when I first read these
words is that the light of Christ within a person was able
to deal with the basic human problem of the ego. But how
did it do this? I could not then derive an answer either from
the text or from my own experience. That nagging question remained with me for twenty years! When I eventually

came to read Barbour's fuller account I began to see an answer. The first thing that struck me was a quotation from Margaret Fell, whom I had thought of, up to that point, as the kindly mother of the Quaker community.

> Now, Friends, deal plainly with yourselves, and let the eternal light search you...for this will deal plainly with you; it will rip you up, and lay you open...naked and bare before the Lord God from whom you cannot hide yourselves....Therefore give over deceiving of your souls.[4]

Barbour comments,

> Here modern experience can recognise the experience of encountering inner truth....The Quaker preachers, like modern psychologists and novelists, knew the many ways the mind can avoid facing unbearable truths.[5]

But facing these truths, if they had the courage to do so, seemed to have a profound effect on people, painful as it may have been, for it exposed the old self as deceitful and made possible the birth of a new, truer self. The person is transformed.

> The same Light that showed them their sins was the source of new life. This may correspond, in modern terminology, to the discovery that the truth is good even when it seems threatening....Another way to think of early Quaker experience is to see it as an example of conversion. In the classic analysis of William James, conversion ends a period of inward conflict of values, when the old ideals or focus of effort is broken down and a new center emerges... More helpful than James' conversion pattern is the

modern psychologist's description of how an old self-image, with its narrow defense mechanisms and ways of self-fulfilment, can be broken open by a period of conflict. In such a breakthrough many previously buried impulses, appreciations, and creative abilities from outside the known limits of the old personality may be released.[6]

I recognised this immediately from my own experience, though still in a limited way. And it began to make sense of the early Quakers' talk of 'the Light'. 'The Light' was a capacity within them to see what they were doing or thinking, while 'the self' was struggling at the same time to keep it well hidden – it wasn't in the interest of the self to acknowledge 'the truth'. If, however, those early Friends accepted the light, then in time, after a period of struggle, this stubborn old self would be deposed and a new self, 'the seed', would come to life within them. This was as far as I could get from reading Barbour's work, and I had many questions about the process he so briefly described, but it was enough to persuade me to read the early Quakers for myself.

By now it was no mere curiosity, though. I was beginning to realise that these early Quakers might well have something to say to my own condition. My own condition was certainly a problem with 'self', or 'ego' as I thought of it. I was dimly aware that my idea of myself didn't entirely fit the reality, that I was having to maintain my self somewhat against the grain of reality, and certainly against the projections and expectations of other people. And here, in the early Quaker writings, I was being told that the first thing I had to do to gain liberation and peace was to face the truth about myself.

2. Finding

But how? I began to read their writings with the hope that I might find the answer to this question. I re-read *Early Quaker Writings*, Fox's *Journal* and, for the first time, Barclay's *Apology*. But what impressed me most were Fox's early tracts and epistles, which I found in the recently reprinted *Works of George Fox*, vols. 1, 4 and 7,[7] the pieces he wrote at the very beginning of the movement, in the 1650s, when he set out to explain what the movement was about and to nurture those people who had already committed themselves to it. These early writings still had a freshness of discovery and freedom of expression, before state persecution and conflict between Friends made him wary and cautious. He made it quite clear then how people were to find the truth that would free them and how they could live their lives on the basis of that truth. In fact, the validity of what he was telling them depended entirely on their being able to access the truth for themselves and test it in their own experience. So his initial message was always the same: give up your dependence on doctrines, rituals, preachers and everything else that is external to you, and find the light within you because that will teach you all you need to know. And you already know what the light is, because it's that that makes you uncomfortable about the things you do wrong. So take note of those uncomfortable feelings, and let 'the light in your conscience' show you what they're all about. If you allow it to, the light will show you the whole truth of your life, and if you then accept that truth, it will set you free – free from guilt and shame, but also free from the powerful desires that made you act wrongly in the first place.

Let me quote at some length from Fox himself, from the tract he wrote in 1653 to articulate the Quaker message for the people of England. Joe Pickvance, who unearthed Fox's original version, called it 'the founding document of the Quaker movement'. The language may be rather difficult for us, though, so I will add my own translation of it into modern English, picking up his allusions to the Bible. (OT = original text. TME = translation into modern English.)

OT

Dwelling in the light, there's no occasion at all of stumbling, for all things are discovered with the light. Thou that lovest it, here's thy teacher, when thou art walking abroad, 'tis present with thee in thy bosom, thou need'st not to say, lo here, or lo there. And as thou liest in thy bed 'tis present to teach thee, and judge thy wandering mind, which would wander abroad, and thy high thoughts and imaginations, and makes them subject; for following thy thoughts thou art quickly lost. But dwelling in this light, it will discover to thee the body of sin, and thy corruptions, and fallen estate where thou art, and multitude of thoughts. In that light which shows thee all this, stand; neither go to the right hand, nor to the left. Here's patience exercised, here's thy will subjected, here thou wilt

TME

So long as you live in the light nothing can trip you up, because you will see everything in the light. Do you love the light? Then here's your teacher! When you are out walking it's there with you, in your heart – you don't have to say 'Look over here', 'Look over there'. And as you lie in bed it's there with you too, teaching you, making you aware of that wandering mind of yours that likes to wander off, and of your attempts to master everything with your own thought and imagination – they themselves are mastered by the light. For if you follow your own thoughts you will soon get lost. But if you live in this light it will reveal to you the root of your wrong-doing, and the distortions of your life, and the degraded condition in which you live, and your endless thinking about everything.

As it shows you all this, stand still, in the light. Don't turn away to the left or the right. This is where you will need to be patient, where your ego will be brought down, where, in what

see the mercies of God made manifest in death. Here thou wilt see the drinking of the waters of Shiloah, which run softly, and the promises of God fulfilled, which are to the Seed, which Seed is Christ. Here thou wilt find a saviour, and the election thou wilt come to know, and the reprobation, which is cast from God, and what enters. He that can own me here, and receive my testimony, into his heart, the immortal Seed is born up, and his own will thrust forth; for it is not him that willeth, nor him that runneth, but the election obtaineth it, and God that shows mercy; for the first step to peace is to stand still in the light (which discovers things contrary to it) for power and strength to stand against that nature which the light discovers. Here grace grows, here's God alone glorified and exalted, and the unknown truth, unknown to the world, made manifest, which draws up that which lies in prison, and refresheth it in time, up to God, out of time, through time.[8]

seems like death to you, you will experience the forgiveness of God. You will experience what it is to drink from 'the waters of Shiloah which flow softly' (Isaiah 8:6), you will see God's promises fulfilled, the promises God made to 'the seed, and the seed refers to Christ' (Galatians 3:16). So here you will find a saviour. You will come to know what it is to be chosen and received by God, and what it is to be rejected, cast away from God.

If you can accept what I am saying here and receive my testimony into your heart, the immortal seed will rise up (within you) as your own will is pushed out. For 'it does not depend on human will or effort, but on God's mercy' (Romans 9:16) – 'the chosen few have attained it' (Romans 11:7).

So the first step to peace is to stand still in the light – the light that reveals whatever is opposed to it. And standing still there you will receive the power and strength to resist that part of you which the light has exposed. Because this is where grace grows, where God alone is seen to be glorious and powerful, and where the unknown truth – unknown to the world out there – is revealed. The truth then liberates what has been held in prison, and in the course of time it revives it, leading it in time to the God who is beyond time.

When I first read this – or perhaps second read it since I didn't find it easy to understand at first! – I was struck by the fact that he was clearly describing a meditative process. He tells his readers that they must learn to control 'thy wandering mind', but not so they could think more noble or rational thoughts, for they, too, 'thy high thoughts and imaginations', have to be brought down. All this internal activity has to stop so that they can 'dwell in the light' in an attitude of passive attention: the light itself, something quite different from their minds, will show them what they need to see. It will show them, among other things, the 'multitude of thoughts' which had previously been blocking their view, but, more importantly, it will show them the 'fallen estate where thou art'. This of course is the truth that they have been trying to hide from themselves, so it will not be easy and it will not be pleasant. The temptation will be to turn away from it, avert their eyes, but Fox advises them explicitly not to do so: 'stand' in the light that shows you all this, he says, 'neither go to the right hand nor to the left. Here's patience exercised.' 'In the light…stand' implies that they don't run away, that they face the truth head on and allow themselves to be thoroughly exposed by the light. But for what purpose? I was at first puzzled by this insistence on baring oneself, even though it takes place in the privacy of meditation. Can people really take so much reality? And won't the effect be to frighten them or depress them? But then I read on and took careful note of the words: 'here's thy will subjected, here thou wilt see the mercies of God made manifest in death'. The point of this exercise is to become aware of the self that likes to assert itself, 'self-will', and likes to pretend that it is all-important, always right, always in control. But when they become aware of the self posturing in this way, it loses its power. It has to submit it to reality: 'here's thy will subjected'. This takes time, of course, to have the pretensions of the self exposed till it eventually submits to reality. In the experience of early Friends this was often a severe, inner struggle, lasting weeks or even months. But once their ego accepted reality, i.e. accepted how they had actually been living their lives, the struggle was over and they experienced peace, a wonderful unimagined peace.

But more than that, they experienced 'mercy' and 'grace', as Fox says here. The collapse of the old ego may seem like death, but 'thou wilt see the mercies of God made manifest in death'. You notice that Fox does not say, 'God will be merciful to you if you repent of your sins', which is what Friends had often heard from the preachers of their day. He says, when you see yourself as you are, in the light, you will also then see the mercy of God, you will experience forgiveness for yourself. So he's telling them of a process they can go through, how they can experience all these wonderful things they have heard about by forgetting what they have heard and following the light in their own troubled conscience. The journey will be difficult, he doesn't hide this fact. Actually he draws attention to it, because he wants them to be ready when they meet difficulty, knowing that if they 'stand' and have patience they will eventually experience liberation from everything they dreaded. Do they really 'know' this? Well, not quite, not yet. They are having to take it on trust. 'He that can own me here, and receive my testimony into his heart, the immortal seed is born up and his own will thrust forth.' He's not appealing to divine authority here, only to his own experience: this promise of a new self that will grow within them as the old self is pushed out, this is Fox's 'testimony' to what he has discovered for himself. But he also claims that if they take his testimony to their hearts and act on it, they will experience the same things that he did.

So he concludes this advice by saying 'The first step to peace is to stand still in the light.' He makes it explicit to them that this is a step-by-step process that they have to undergo if they want to find peace, and that standing still in the face of difficult truths about their life is only the first step.

My discovery of this process in the early writings of Fox was very thrilling for me. It opened up the whole meaning of the first Quaker witness, and it also suggested to me how I might benefit from this teaching myself, because it was telling me something I could *do* to gain the insight I was after. But first I had to read more of Fox and other early writers to see if I had understood them correctly, and to see what implications might follow from this. Fox himself was never easy to read, I found, but I was determined to master his language and follow the nuances of what he was saying. So I took two years to read through the eight volumes of his collected *Works*, checking out the language with historical dictionaries and the 'authorised version' of the English Bible, which Fox himself (mostly) used.[9]

It became clear from this study that the meditative process was thought of as the basis for a whole way of life. To be sure, truth had to be accessed through a discipline of silence and waiting, but once it had been 'seen' and accepted it had to be acted on. Then more insight would be gained, and one's own life would become richer and more effective. One would gain a clear sense of God as the source of truth and being, and a clear insight into the lives of other people, from which love and unity would then be possible. In fact the experience of love and unity between the Friends of Truth would be a great source of strength for each individual Friend. For each on their own was limited, unable to respond fully to the light, so they needed one another to make up what was lacking. In those first, small meetings together, when they 'waited in the light', they would share their experiences of the light and support one another in difficulty. But what they did when they sat in silence together was essentially the same as what they did on their own: they waited for the truth of their lives to be revealed to them, and afterwards, whether alone or together, they acted in obedience to the truth revealed.

Another thing that impressed me in reading Fox was that he urged Friends to act on the truth so that other people could see it, too. It wasn't only for their own benefit. If they cared for others they would want them to know the joy and freedom that comes from truth, but that truth cannot be conveyed adequately in words because it is the truth of people's lives which they each have to experience for themselves. Some other way must be found, and Fox's extraordinary insight is that if people live their lives in accordance with the truth that has been disclosed to them in the light, their lives will then bear witness to the truth and touch the hearts of other people. 'Blessed be the Lord', he said with some excitement, 'the truth is reached in the hearts of people beyond words.'[10]

There was even a hope that if enough people responded to truth then society itself would change. It would shift from a reliance on fear and force as a basis for order to mutual trust. So Friends' own commitment to non-violence in the resolution of conflict would so affect people's understanding of reality, their own reality in particular, that they would want to embrace non-violence too. Friends described their 'peace declaration' of 1660 as a

OT	**TME**
testimony unto all the world of the truth of our hearts in this	*confident declaration to the whole world of the truth of our hearts in*

particular, that as God per-
suadeth every man's heart to
believe, so they may receive it.[11]

this case, in the hope that they receive it as God persuades everyone's heart to accept it.

That was not a wholly unrealistic expectation, because the people of Europe at that time were profoundly disillusioned by the political regimes which had relied on force and violence to establish themselves: they were open to change. But the change offered by Friends was perhaps too radical for most, certainly for those still holding on to power. So Friends' hopes were soon disappointed. The 'day of the Lord' did not come in their lifetime. But even with the failure of their grand mission, their testimony still remained valid, if not now as a model for immediate change, then as a witness to what is ultimately possible when people are ready for it. So their mission became more modest: to gather and sustain people who were prepared to put their faith in truth and to live their lives together in faithful obedience to it.

This was the understanding I acquired from reading more widely in early Friends and it seemed to me to make sense of the whole Quaker project. But I also realised that in trying to understand what they said and did I had to give up the idea that what held it all together was some *idea*! I had been unable to find any belief that early Quakers held in common as the basis for their faith, not even the belief that there was 'that of God' in everyone. To them 'that of God' in people represented not a belief but an experience, the experience of light within themselves in the first instance, and then an experience of the divine source in others as they opened their hearts to them. So the basis of early Quaker faith and life was something very immediate, personal and practical. They turned in meditation to the divine source of life within them and then lived their lives simply in response to that. This was not a belief but a practice, and it was surprisingly simple. And that applied as much to their grand hopes for changing the world as it did to their desire to seek change in their own lives.

So what was this simple practice? I needed to focus more sharply on that in order to make better sense of the whole, and to find the nugget of wisdom I was looking for in my own life. Fox, I found, was more clear about this than any of the others, perhaps because he was the one who had explored this most fully in his own experience. We have looked at an early account of the practice in that tract of his from 1653, *To all that would know the way to the kingdom*. But that is not all he had to say on the matter: most of the 200 tracts and epistles of those first ten years have something to say about it. In Epistle 10 (1652), for example, he gives advice on how to deal with temptation, and you will notice how, again, he recommends a step-by-step process.

OT	**TME**
Whatever ye are addicted to, the tempter will come in that thing; and when he can trouble you, then he gets advantage over you, and then ye are gone. Stand still in that which is pure, after ye see yourselves; and then mercy comes in. After thou seest thy thoughts, and the temptations, do not think, but submit; and then power comes. Stand still in that which shows and discovers; and there doth strength immediately come. And stand	*Whatever it is you are addicted to that's where the tempter will get you. If he can trouble you there he gets an advantage over you, and then you are finished. So see what's happening to you, what you are doing, then wait there in the light of what is pure in you, and you will find forgiveness. When you have seen what's going on in your mind, and the temptations there, do not think, just submit (to reality). You will then receive power. If you stand still in that (light) that exposes and reveals, you will find that strength is immediately given to*

still in the light, submit to it, and the other will be hushed and gone; and then content comes....Your strength is to stand still, after ye see your-selves.[12]

you. So, stand still in the light, submit to it, and all the rest will quieten down or disappear. You will then be contented....Your strength is to stand still, once you have seen yourselves.

We have three steps here: 1. see yourselves in the light, 2. stand still in the light, 3. submit to the light. Then mercy comes and power and strength, but these don't count as 'steps' because they come as a gift. They are not human actions. The human action in the process is surprisingly non-active, though: see, stand still, submit. To these three we need to add a fourth, which is the step that gets the process going, and it is always Fox's first advice: Mind the light, i.e. pay attention to it. So let us look at these four steps in turn. We shall see later on that we today might have some difficulty with them, but first of all we need to under-stand what early Friends had in mind and what in fact they did when they sat down in silence for an hour or two. When we understand that we shall better understand what they were doing with the rest of their time, engaging with one another and the world in general. This time of silence and waiting was the basis for all the rest. Unfortunately, they never tell us what they did in the silence in a system-atic way, setting out all the steps and explaining what each entailed, but they do give us enough clues to piece it together for ourselves. So here is an attempt to do just that.[13] I shall use as headings phrases they used themselves to describe the process. The first step is to:

(1) Mind the light

OT

TME

Mind the pure light of God in you, which shows you sin and

Pay attention to the pure light of God in you. It is this that makes you aware evil, and how you have spent your time, and shows you how your minds go forth.[14]

of what you have done wrong, how you have (mis)spent your time, and how your minds have projected (on to things outside).

So Fox in 1654. 'Let the light of Jesus Christ, that shines in every one of your consciences, search you thoroughly, and it will let you clearly see.'[15] Fox again, indicating what the light would do and why we need it – that takes us into steps 2 and 3 in fact – but his first point is to make possible the work of God in our hearts by paying attention to the light. That may seem like simple advice, but to carry it out is often far from simple, as Fox well knew. For example, what is this light we are supposed to give attention to? It is not immediately obvious. But Fox tells us where to look: 'the light…that shines in everyone of your consciences', 'the light which shows you sin and evil'. We are well aware of our conscience. We have only to stop and consider if there is anything in our lives we feel uncomfortable about and we can feel a twinge or niggle about something or other. This simple, everyday experience is the starting point of the Quaker journey. Start with yourself, they are saying, with your present situation, identify whatever it is in your life that you already feel uneasy about and take a look at it. Does that mean the light *is* the conscience? I don't think so, though sometimes it sounds like it. Early Friends all make a point of referring to the light *in* their conscience, implying that it was something distinct. And I take the difference to be this: your conscience makes you feel good or bad about things you've done, and the light then shows you precisely what those things are. The function of the light is to show you what's really happening: 'the light is that by which ye come to see',[16] 'for with the light man sees himself'.[17]

But why do we need the light to show us what we are doing wrong, or doing right for that matter? Surely we know all this already? Not really, according to early Friends. We think we do, but that is because we tell ourselves (and others) stories about what we do, to fit in with the way we want to think of ourselves and the way we want to be thought of. It is a form of deceit, strictly speaking, though it is often well-meant. And it won't help us to think about this so as to correct the story; our thinking and our imagining are too bound up with our self-interest, our ego-needs, so they will always bend things for the purpose. We need to stop thinking and stop telling stories, then another kind of awareness will come to the fore, led by a concern for things in our lives that are not quite right, and it will let us see what's going on behind all the images and stories. We have to give our attention to that kind of awareness. Then we can take the next step.

(2) Open your heart to the truth

The advice here could be 'see yourself in the light', as Fox describes it in Epistle 10, for that is exactly what we have to do. We have to see ourselves with the kind of awareness that comes into play when we stop doing things and stop thinking. But it is not a matter of simply looking. There are obstacles to our seeing ourselves, which arise mostly from within us: there is fear, for example, anxiety, pride, and our attachment to the idea we already have of ourselves. So what we need to concentrate on at this point is letting go of that idea, and being open to reality. 'Stand all naked, bare and uncovered before the Lord', says Fox,[18] intending it metaphorically of course! He's saying, be open, be honest, be straight with yourself and with God. And that requires courage and determination, because the temptation is always there to cover things up if we don't like them, to clothe ourselves in a desirable and acceptable self-image.

This doesn't mean that we have to set about analysing ourselves until we get to the basic reality. In this process analysing won't help very much. We have simply to be open to whatever is presented to us, ready to see the coverings fall away and to have the truth revealed to us. It is an attitude of receptivity. This is why silence is so important. It enables the normal activities of the ego to subside, and to allow the words and images that normally preoccupy us to drop away. Silence and stillness seem to be the physical preconditions for an attitude of mind that is completely open.

(3) Wait in the light

Or 'stand still in the light', which comes to the same thing. There is a process to be gone through here, many things might happen, and it will certainly take time. Remember Fox says 'The first step to peace is to stand still in the light',[19] rather than run away, implying that this first step can be difficult and rough. Well, this is not surprising, for this particular way to peace starts with the negativity. We are to begin by looking at what *disturbs* our peace, the conflict and agitation, so that eventually we can overcome these things. So 'here patience is exercised', as he says in the same passage. In the meditation that will mean that when we are made aware of the bad things in our life we look at them squarely in the face, we take in the full reality of what is going on there. If that seems impossible think about this: if we see them 'in the light' we won't get bogged down in them, because we won't be trying to solve these problems with our own plans, arguments and practical devices. We will simply be looking at them in a detached manner, without interference from the ego. There is then a kind of distance between us and the problem. And being aware of that distance is itself very encouraging, because we realise we are not entangled by the problem anymore. For the time being at least, we are free of it. In fact, being able to see the matter that has been troubling us, and to see it whole, as it really is, this gives us a new ability eventually to deal with it. So already the situation is changing. Simply seeing things in the light and waiting patiently as the reality of the situation sinks in, gives us a power to act which we didn't have before. Listen to this advice from Fox to Lady Claypool, a daughter of Oliver Cromwell, who was very depressed and unhappy at the time:

OT

Be still and cool in thy own mind and spirit from thy own thoughts, and then thou wilt feel the principle of God to turn thy mind to the Lord God, whereby thou wilt receive his strength and power from whence life comes, to allay all tempests, against blusterings and storms....What the light doth make manifest and discover, temptations, confusions, distractions, distempers: do not look at the temptations, confusions, corruptions, but at the light that discovers them, that makes them manifest; and with the same light you will feel over them, to receive power to stand against them....That will give victory; and you will find grace and strength; and there is the first step to peace.[20]

TME

Be still and cool in your own mind and spirit from your own thoughts, and you will then feel the divine source of life in you turn your mind to the Lord God. And in doing this you will receive his strength and life-giving power to quieten every storm and gale that blows against you....When the light discloses and reveals things to you, things that tempt you, confuse you, distract you and the like, don't go on looking at them, but look at the light that has made you aware of them. And with this same light you will feel yourself rising above them and empowered to resist them....That enables you to overcome them, and you will find grace and strength. And there is the first step to peace.

You see that Fox is inviting her to undertake a meditation in which she will experience a profound change. She is depressed, so he tells her to begin by looking at what depresses her, allowing the light to 'uncover' the situation and not engaging with her 'own thoughts' about it. When she has seen her situation for what it is she is to turn her gaze from those dark and troubling realities to the light that has made them visible; i.e. she is to become aware of the new situation arising in the meditation itself. She had been *in* that dark reality, overwhelmed by it, but now, having allowed the light to show her the truth about it, she is *out* of it. Simply by seeing things as they are she is connected with something outside her troubled ego which is pure, truthful, all-seeing, unaffected by the troubles of the world, yet, she will discover, is merciful and compassionate and powerful. She is connected with 'that of God' in her, the divine source of life, the Christ within.

But this happy realisation isn't quite the end of the process. If Elizabeth Claypool is to benefit from this divine source she has discovered within her, she must, finally,

(4) Submit to the truth

That was made explicit in Epistle 10, remember:

OT	TME
After thou seest thy thoughts, and the temptations, do not think, but submit; and then power comes....Stand still in the light, submit to it, and the other [the temptation] will be hushed and gone.[21]	*When you have seen what's going on in your mind, and the temptations there, do not think, just submit (to reality). You will then receive power....So, stand still in the light, submit to it, and all the rest will quieten down or disappear.*

What does this mean? 'Submit' is not a comfortable word for us moderns, not even if it means submitting to

God. Well, note the wording carefully. It doesn't say submit to God, but submit to the light. Submitting to God could well mean, as it does for some Christians, giving up responsibility and intellectual integrity and accepting the dictates of the heavenly Father. Submitting to the light implies none of that, since to benefit from the light you have to look and see for yourself, and in that sense *take* responsibility for your situation. But once you have done that and seen the truth you have to accept the truth, acknowledge it, give up the stories you have been telling yourself and all the other forms of self-deception you have indulged in. Seeing is not enough, so long as you are secretly holding on to your ideas of who you are and what your situation is. 'Do not think but submit.' If you go on thinking, despite what you have seen, you will continue to experience conflict within yourself, and misery, and your customary inability to act decisively. But 'submit' to reality and that conflict will be over: your life will be integrated in this acceptance of reality, and you will experience peace, contentment, well-being.

Of course, ultimately, submission to reality is submission to God, since God is the ultimate reality. And being at peace with ourselves we find peace with God. But along this path to God we do not have to surrender our intellect, our feeling for life, our morality, our integrity, our sense of truth. On the contrary, they make up the path.

3. Testing

I could not doubt, when I read the letters and journals of early Friends, that they had experienced the process that Fox described. And the pattern was often the same. They would be troubled in their consciences, perhaps as a result of hearing a Quaker preach, and as they opened themselves to the reality of what they had done or were doing they felt their whole life exposed. Something within them was revealing the truth about their life. Thomas Ellwood wrote, 'The general trouble and confusion of mind, which had for some days lain heavy upon me and pressed me down, without a distinct discovery of the particular cause for which it came, began now to wear off, and some glimmerings of light began to break forth in me, which let me see my inward state and condition towards God....Now was all my former life ripped up.'[22] This is what they meant by being 'convinced' by God's spirit within them. But in response to all this the 'self' would protest, and there would then follow a period of struggle between the self and the spirit that could last for days or weeks, or even months. Eventually, though, they would yield and they would allow the spirit or 'the seed' to rule their lives. And then, with the conflict over, they would experience great peace and joy.[23]

I could not say the same for myself, though, not yet. If anything, my reading of the early Quakers had made me even more aware than I was already of the conflicts in my life that remained unresolved. I knew that there was a depth to my experience which could not be accounted for simply by my conscious self and the various thoughts and desires that surfaced there, but I couldn't say that I knew this depth intimately or had confidence in it. There was still too much fear and anxiety about what it might contain.

So I decided to try out for myself the meditative practice I had discovered in early Friends. I put aside half an hour each day – this was back in 1995, later I was to give more time to it – to follow the pattern as best I could. After some relaxation exercises, I allowed myself to become aware of anything that was troubling my mind, anything that seemed to come from the depth and made me uncomfortable about how I was living my life. This part wasn't so difficult! But then I tried to focus on the reality of this uncomfortable thing, relaxing in the silence and trying to pay attention: this part was not so easy. There were so many distractions, so many voices in my head responding to this troubling presence that I could hardly concentrate on the thing itself. But with some patience I began to get a sense of what was going on in my life which was quite different from what I wanted to say or think about it. Inevitably I had to focus on those two relationships that were bothering me. With one, a younger man, I could make no progress, because my feelings were too strong – I did not yet know how to be 'still and cool in my own mind from my own thoughts'. But with the other I had a startling experience. I was already aware, as I've said, that I wasn't being entirely honest with my friend because I sensed it could spoil the relationship we had. But when I allowed myself to face the reality of my relationship with her I could see that I was not even being honest with myself. I was not allowing myself to recognise or acknowledge what I was in fact experiencing. So I hardly knew my own feelings – what I really felt about her, what I wanted, what I felt about the differences between us. All this was partly obscured by what she felt, because, I discovered, I was anxious to please her and not to offend. I was so unsure of myself that I wanted to know first where she stood, so that I could then find out where I should stand. But I never did find out, since I was not fully aware of my own feelings. This is why I was stuck, and unhappy, and this is why we had our 'misunderstandings'. But as I meditated on this bleak situation two words came to me, out of the blue: 'be real'. I understood immediately how I had got into this situation and how I could get out of it. 'Of course', I said to myself, 'I have been acting a part, and in a script largely written by other people. But that has been my whole life! No wonder I found it difficult to know myself. And no wonder I have difficulties in my relation-ships. Yet, all I need to do is "be real", and none of this will happen. The choice is mine. It's only a matter of courage, and acceptance, and I can be free. No, knowing this now I am free!'

This was my liberation, or the beginning of it. The rela-tionship improved from that very day. Changes that I feared would happen if I 'spoke my mind' did happen, but the relationship became more real as a result, more lucid, trusting and spontaneous. What had been threatened in my imagination was only the idea I had of myself, this false, unrealistic self, and it did me the world of good to be rid of it.

But more than this, I had discovered for myself that the process worked. I told my story to a friend of mine who was also a psychotherapist. She was impressed. 'But isn't it strange,' I said, 'that the first Quakers found a therapeutic process which didn't need a therapist, and that nobody seems to have noticed, or discovered the process for them-selves?' 'Yes,' she said, 'but have you read Eugene Gendlin?' 'Who?' 'Gendlin. He's an American psychologist at the University of Chicago who writes about a process very similar to the one you are describing. It's in his book *Focusing*.' Indeed it was, though it took me nearly a year to find the book and then to get round to reading it. And the process he described was indeed similar to the one I had discovered and experienced myself. This was surprising, but it was the more surprising that he had arrived at it in the course of his studies as an academic psychologist and not, as I had, in pursuit of spiritual enlightenment. His par-ticular concern as a professional was the effectiveness of psychotherapy. In his wide-ranging studies of the practice of psychotherapy he had been struck by the fact that what made a particular practice successful was not the method employed or the theory behind it, not even the skill of the therapist, but the ability of the client to make a connection with his or her present state of being. It did not so much matter either what a client talked about. 'The difference is in *how* they talk. And that is only an outward sign of the real difference: *what the successful patients do inside themselves.*'[24] They would talk in a hesitant way – Gendlin and his colleagues had studied hundreds of tapes of therapy in session – groping for the words to describe a feeling or sense they had at that moment. When they acknowledged that feeling, and named it, and came to see what it was all about, then they began to make progress. Gendlin could see the immense value of this, not merely for therapists and their clients, but for everyone and anyone who had personal problems, anyone who was 'stuck, cramped, hemmed in, slowed down'.[25] So he found a way to teach this 'skill', as he called it, of making a connection with one's own inner being. This is where the similarity with early Friends becomes most apparent. He devised a six-step guide which would take people through a process of self-discovery in a quite short period of time. But there was nothing automatic about this; he would be teaching people to do something which, though simple in itself, might be very difficult to learn. 'The internal equipment needed to perform the act is in every human being, but in most people it is unused. A few seem to use it intuitively now and then, but the chances are you have never deliberately done it and have never been aware the possibility exists….Some people learn this inner way fairly fast, while others need some weeks or months of patient inner listening and tinkering.'[26]

Let me quote from his own summary of the six-step guide so that you can see how it both agrees with and differs from the Quaker process – although that first impression of difference, I suspect, may turn out to be misleading.

1. **Clearing a space**. What I will ask you to do [is to] be silent.…All right – now, inside you, I would like you to pay attention inwardly in your body, perhaps in your stomach or chest. Now see what comes *there* when you ask, 'How is my life going? What is the main thing for me right now?' Sense within your body. Let the answers come slowly from this sensing. When some concern comes, *do not go inside it*. Stand back, say 'Yes, that's there. I can feel that there.' Let there be a little space between you and that. Then ask what else you feel. Wait again, and sense. Usually there are several things.

2. **Felt sense**. From among what came, select one personal problem to focus on. Do not go inside it. Stand back from it. Of course, there are many parts to that one thing you are thinking about – too many to think of each one alone. But you can feel all of these things together. Pay attention there where you usually feel things, and in there you can get a sense of what *all of the problem* feels like.…

3. **Handle**. What is the quality of this unclear felt sense? Let a word, a phrase, or an image come up from the felt sense itself.…

4. **Resonating**. Go back and forth between the felt sense and the word (phrase or image). Check how they resonate with each other.…

5. **Asking**. Now ask: What is it about this whole problem that makes this quality (which you have just named or pictured)?…Be with the felt sense till something comes along with a [bodily] shift, a slight 'give' or release.

6. **Receiving**. Receive whatever comes with a shift in a friendly way.[27]

I found it quite possible to carry out these instructions merely from reading the book, though I discovered afterwards that that was unusual, since most people who do 'focusing' have learnt it from a qualified teacher. But I was half-way there, of course, having practised something similar already. So as soon as I tried it I found I could do it, and also that it worked for me. I became aware of things about myself that had previously been obscure. It seemed to combine well with what I was already doing, and even to deepen it. Why was this? It was not a particularly spiritual practice. In fact, I attended one workshop on focusing where I learnt how to gain a 'felt sense' of what I really wanted for breakfast! But if I chose to take it deeper, I could. I could focus on an emotional problem, or a difficulty with someone at work, or my creative block in writing. It made sense to think of 'focusing' as a tool or a skill which can be put to many different uses, practical, creative, moral, emotional or spiritual.

I tried it once in relation to a family gathering. Christmas was coming and I found I was anxious about the impending family get-together, which in the past had often become argumentative and acrimonious. So I took this feeling into the light, to see what it was about. I could feel it physically in my stomach. 'What's going on here?', I asked, and an image arose in my mind, rather like an actual memory of past Christmas gatherings, where everyone in my family was clamouring for attention. That was already a new insight. I had only seen the surface behaviour, but now behind it I began to sense their need. 'Why is everyone clamouring for attention?' I waited for an answer, without trying to answer the question myself. And sure enough, I received an image of them gathered in a circle, each asking for love from the others. And I was asking for love, too. I knew what I had to do: to be aware of their needs, and to offer what love I could in response. That Christmas I was light-hearted and cheerful.

I also tried to gain insight into this one relationship that still troubled me, where my feelings had been too strong to meditate before. I was encouraged now by my positive experiences, and with the skill of focusing I was more able to keep a distance and see things objectively. This person was unaccountably aggressive towards me, yet he needed my help, or so I felt. But when I brought my concern to the light for clarification the situation changed. What I saw – it was again a strong memory-like image – was a vulnerable man, full of frustration with himself and with life, longing to love and be loved. I saw this as intimately as if I was two feet away from him. My heart opened to him and tears streamed down my face. My own fear of his aggression disappeared and with it the 'veil' that had covered my eyes, that prevented me seeing him as he really was. I have never felt the same about him since: my love has been unfrozen.

It is clear from these experiences that more was needed on my part than the use of a mere skill. There had to be the desire for wholeness and healing, a readiness to face truth that might be painful, and a willingness to let go my ego which so likes to think it has the answers already. I had to accept my own need, and my dependence on a source of light and life beyond the known limits of my everyday self. But when at last I was able to do this, I was glad to have learnt this psychological skill. It enabled me to make a connection with that part of myself that I did not really know, and to 'hear' what it had to say. I think Ann Weiser Cornell is right when she says that when you listen to this deeper sense within you, 'you are allowing yourself to be open to the depth and richness of your whole self....Focusing is the process of listening to your body in a gentle, accepting way and hearing the messages that your inner self is sending you. It's a process of honouring the wisdom that you have inside you, becoming aware of the subtle level of knowing that speaks to you through your body.'[28] And I can believe her when she says 'focusing is the fastest way I know to get to the truth of ourselves and to live it.'[29]

So the newly discovered skill of focusing can be put to spiritual use, and might be an important resource for people like Quakers who want to get in touch with a source of wisdom and guidance within them which lies beyond the reach of their normal mental processes. This is the least we could say. But we could also say that focusing is partly a rediscovery of what at least the early Quakers had already found. Certainly they were able to do precisely what Gendlin and Cornell are recommending, and some more besides. Why then, if we have this heritage, should we bother with focusing? I have asked this question frequently as I have experimented with Quaker meditation by myself and with other Quakers too. Theoretically, we shouldn't need other helps because 'the light of Christ within' is sufficient. But practically, we do need help because, as I've found myself, we have difficulty in accessing the light and in keeping in touch with it. Many Friends have told me that they have tried to do what I described, from early Quaker practice, but failed. They could not relax enough, they could not stop thinking or wandering off in their minds, they could not interpret the images or words that came up in the meditation, or they could not distinguish the various voices in their heads. We must be familiar with all this merely from the practice of sitting in silence to ponder something important. Our modern minds are simply not tuned to the 'voice of truth' within. And it *is* a matter of modernity, I believe.

In contrast to traditional ways of living, modernity relies on what we can consciously think about and talk about, what we can demonstrate or exhibit in the public arena. We moderns need to be in control. That is our strength. But it is also our weakness, because we dare not trust those aspects of our life that elude our control, our rational understanding. We become insensitive to them, even sometimes denying their very existence. Inhabiting only the conscious part of ourselves we lose touch with the unconscious part. Living in our heads we become estranged from our bodies, thinking of them only as material things that exist for our use or enjoyment. Our minds therefore need always to be busy, to be occupied, trying either to control the world or to squeeze some pleasure from it. This modern mind of ours does not like to be quiet, still, receptive. It does not like to be empty. When emptiness or silence threatens it seeks to protect itself with images, words and sounds.

I say all this, not so much to slight the modern world, as to explain why we Quakers, who are moderns too, have such difficulty with our own spiritual practice. The early Quakers did not have these difficulties, apparently. When told to be silent and 'mind the light in their consciences', they were quite able to do this; I've found no record of anyone who couldn't.[30] And they could do this for hours on end, especially when they met together 'in the silent assemblies of God's people'. Why was it possible for them and not for us? I can only think that our modern minds are so full of words and images, imported mostly from outside, not least from TV and the media, that there is no room left for silence and emptiness. We have so developed the skill of manipulating words and images that we have lost the skill of simply paying attention.

But that skill can be learned. We have 'the equipment', as Gendlin says, though it lies largely unused. We must learn to use it again, and that is where focusing can help. It can help, I suggest, in four specific ways:

1 by paying attention first of all to the sensations in our body so that we can get out of our heads into another way of experiencing, and that we can become aware of what is troubling us deep down – the body seems to register these deeper conflicts within us;

2 by asking questions of ourselves, or rather of the light within us, and deliberately not answering them with our conscious minds – this helps us to go beyond the limits of our conscious thinking and to open ourselves to the reality we need to know;

3 by allowing a word or image to arise from this deeper awareness that convincingly expresses what it is about – this not only sharpens our awareness of the situation we are concerned with, but gives us a 'password' to visit it in meditation on other occasions;

4 by giving time to welcome the insights that come to us, so that we can absorb them and integrate them into our experience and dispel the images we have hitherto relied on for lack of the real thing – this saying 'yes' to reality is effectively 'submitting to the truth'.

4. Sharing

This was certainly effective in my own case. I found it possible to look at any aspect of my life that was causing me concern and to find a way through, that is, to find at least the next step I should take in dealing with it. But this work on myself over a number of issues had a profounder effect on me than I had anticipated. Almost every issue I looked at shed light on me and how I was choosing to relate to the issue. I found I was looking at myself as if from a point outside me, and I became sharply aware of the image I had of myself, the image I had had for many years, and in some shape or form for the whole of my life. In one meditation I was becoming conscious of this strong self-image, and I asked of the light, 'What is this ego of mine?' And the response was a picture of an egg, a hard, but brittle egg. I was awe-struck by this. It fitted so exactly what I knew about myself, deep down, but never had the courage or wit to accept. My sense of self was tightly formed, as close to an ideal as I could manage, and yet held together by a shell – not its own inner strength – which could presumably break quite easily. What was this shell? Why was it so hard? I put this to the light, realising I was already out of my depth but needing the insight desperately. No picture came, just a word: 'fear'. Fear was holding my self-image together, and fear was cutting it off from all the rest of me, and from other people. The 'egg' now seemed to be floating in space, isolated and alone. At first I was very troubled by this – at the shame and stupidity of it. But then I noticed that the fear itself was no longer there. Here I was, looking directly at my fragile self, and I was not afraid. On the contrary, I was quietly confident that since I was facing the truth I would be okay. More than that, by simply looking honestly at what I was, I was connecting with something much bigger than me, bigger than this puny self that thought it was everything, or at least everything that mattered. I was not *inside* that self anymore, looking at the world as something out there. I was outside, free from its narrow confines, but grounded in reality, reconciled to it, at one with it. Free in myself, and yet one with everything! I am already in contradiction trying to describe it.

Needless to say, the old fearful ego soon began to assert itself again, but the experience inspired in me a much deeper trust in the light than I had had before. The fear that had kept me isolated and apart, or rather made me feel that way, could now be faced in the silence and stillness and the light would melt it again. (I playfully thought of my 'self' as a snowman that was constructed in a cold, hard world, but which soon melted away when the sun came out.) The meditative practice I had been experimenting with now became very simple. I had simply to be still and quiet until the activity of my everyday self subsided and I could be open to the guidance of a deeper self that would show me what I needed to know and prompt me on what I needed to do.

It began to dawn on me that I had at last found what I had been looking for all these years. But not in the way I had expected to. I had expected, or at least hoped, to find an idea, an interpretation of Quaker faith that I could then put into practice. But it came the other way round. I found a practice, and out of this arose the faith. Not that I produced the faith myself, for the practice was and is a matter of opening myself to what is already there, receiving what is offered, responding to what is revealed to me. The faith was produced in me by something much deeper in me than my conscious ego, but something that made itself felt by twinges of conscience that told me that all was not well with me. As I responded to these and allowed myself to be shown what was really going on in my life, I became aware of the self-deceptions that made me think that 'I', this conscious ego, was the centre of my being and of my world – and aware of the truth, that my life was rooted in a reality way beyond my ken, but a reality that I could nevertheless trust. I had to use the word 'God' to signal this other-than-me which gave me my being, though I was aware intellectually of the impossibility of using the word in a logically consistent way. Paradoxical though it would be, I had to say that God was the source of my new-found freedom and joy.

One of the questions I had put to myself at the beginning of this search was whether my Quaker faith was deep enough and powerful enough to deal with the personal crises I was living through. At the time, I had to confess, it was not. But now, after a time of struggle, I could say that it was. And it wasn't just my faith that had grown strong, it was Quaker faith. That is, I had come to discover in my experience how deep and powerful the Quaker faith really was. My eyes had been opened to the richness of this one tradition, when I had thought it was relatively poor. What I had to do now was clear. I had to share my experience and understanding with others. In particular, I had to tell Quakers what I had found in our Quaker tradition, the riches of spiritual insight and experience that could surely enrich us again today. But there were questions in my mind, too. How much of what I had found was applicable only to me? Was my understanding of it relevant to other Quakers? And would the meditative process work for them as it had for me? Especially in the modern form I had come to use for myself? What would have to change? These questions could be answered, I realised, only in the sharing of what I had found. So the sharing, the communication, would have to be experimental too, an extension of the open experiment I had begun on myself.

One of the first attempts to communicate my new understanding was at a meeting of German Friends in April 1996.[31] I had been asked to give a talk to the Northwest Gathering of Friends at Bad Pyrmont on the theme of 'Quaker identity', following the publication of my book *Wo Worte enden*.[32] What I suggested in that talk, to put it very briefly, was that to rediscover who we as Quakers are we need to recover the meaning of our distinctive practice. For what gave us our identity was not a common set of beliefs, but a common practice: waiting in silence, being open to leading, refusing to use violence, and so on. So I described the practice of the very first Quakers, explaining why they did what they did, and suggested how we might develop that practice today. I thought my explanation would be enough to convince Friends. I suggested to the groups which were to meet after the lecture that they consider the question, 'Is this practice of early Friends relevant today?' When they reported back to the meeting as a whole, one Friend said, 'Our group couldn't answer this question. How can we know whether the practice is relevant unless we try it?' I was taken aback by this reply. It was obviously right, and I said so at the time, but at that point I had nothing more to suggest about what they might do.

I took that question home with me and thought about it for some months. I couldn't expect Friends to see the relevance of the practice merely from listening to me talk about it. They had to try it for themselves. And that is what the practice itself requires: each person must discover the light for themselves, within them, as it illuminates the problems in their own personal lives. But how are they to do this? Was it enough to explain what early Friends had done and invite them to do the same? Possibly, but I had tried that myself and found it too difficult, at least to begin with. Could I then tell them of my own experiments and my discovery of a new, modern way of 'waiting in the light'? Yes, that would be better, but better still if I could take them through the meditation there and then, so we could do it together and then reflect on the experience afterwards. What was needed was a workshop format: a day or a weekend devoted to the practice, when we had time to do everything that needed to be done and to say everything that needed to be said. I had been to workshops and knew how helpful they could be in enabling people to learn from experience, though I had never given a workshop myself. It felt like another risky experiment – this time on other people! – but it seemed right to try.

I tried first at a General Meeting of Friends in England, in September of that year (1996). After talking about the early Quaker experience I invited the 120 or so Friends who were there to try an 'experiment with light' to see if they could experience the light as the early Quakers had. I used the fourfold pattern I had found in their writings as a basis – mind the light, open your heart, wait in the light, and submit to the truth. I then combined it with some advice of Eugene Gendlin on focusing, the advice I had found particularly helpful in my own experience. The result was a six-step guide to Quaker meditation which was to last 30 minutes – later I expanded it to 40 minutes when I realised that more time was needed. Each step was to last five minutes. A couple of sentences would be read, and then there would be silence while Friends tried to follow the advice given. The steps were briefly as follows – I am quoting from the text I used at the time (the full text of the meditation guide is given in the Appendix, '1. the individual').

1. **Relax body and mind**....Let yourself become wholly receptive. (Five minutes silence.)

2. In this receptive state of mind, **let the real concerns of your life emerge**. Ask yourself, 'What is really going on in my life?', but do not try to answer the question...(silence).

3. Now **focus on one issue** that presents itself, one thing that gives you a sense of unease. And try to get a sense of this thing as a whole....

4. Now ask yourself **why it is like that**....Wait in the light till you see what it is. Let the answer come.

5. When the answer comes **welcome it**....Trust the light. Say yes to it. Submit to it....It will show you the way through.

6. As soon as you accept what is being revealed to you,
   you will begin to **feel different**....Accepting truth
   about yourself is like making peace.

You will recognise the fourfold pattern in this, and also
the way I was trying to cope with difficulties that arise for
us moderns. But notice, too, the process of 'focusing down'.
You are advised to begin by noting anything and everything
in your life that causes you some concern, that is, the things
that come to mind when you ask in a relaxed state of mind,
'what is really going on in my life?' Having made a check-
list, as it were, you then select one issue to focus on –
ideally you try to see what issue is asking to be attended to.
Your mind is like a movie camera that focuses down on the
interesting detail and records precisely what's going on
there. When you become aware of that, you focus down
again to see what's making this happen, and that usually
reveals something about yourself that needs to be faced and
accepted. So the next step is precisely to face it and accept
it. Finally, you notice how you feel, having gone through all
that, because that tells you whether the issue has been
resolved, at least as far as you are concerned. If it has been,
you will feel remarkably good, however bad the issue itself
might have been. You will have found some peace.

That was the intention of the process. The result at that
meeting of Friends was tangible. It was evident from their
faces, many of them with tears, that some of them had been
deeply affected. Others stood up to say they had gained
insight or clarity on an issue that greatly concerned them.
They asked if we could meet again in the free time and do
the meditation once more, this time with space to share our
experiences more fully. So after lunch 34 Friends met in a
crowded loft and we went through the six-step process
once again. One or two were clearly having difficulty, but
most of them gained something of real value. I clearly

remember two Friends who recounted their experience. One said that relations at work were bad and had been for the 15 years she had been working there. But now the light had shown her what was really going on and she realised what she could do to change matters. For the first time in 15 years she felt free of the burden of that place. Another woman talked about her new Meeting where she didn't feel at all at home. It seemed she was being cold-shouldered. But all she got in the silence were the words, 'you are being defensive' and she couldn't understand what that had to do with it. What followed next surprised me. A couple of other Friends suggested to her that what she 'heard' in the meditation was significant because it explained why she was getting a cold response. 'Oh', she said, '*I'm* being too defensive so *they* can't get close to me? Now I see.' I learnt from this that Friends could help one another in understanding what the light is showing them.

As I walked back home from that meeting I realised that I had to devote myself to this work. It *was* possible to teach this practice, it *did* help people to open to the light, and, surprisingly, they could help one another to understand it. I travelled widely in the next three years – in Britain and many countries of Europe – to give lectures, talks and workshops to communicate the understanding and teach the practice. Friends throughout Europe seemed very eager to hear about this and to try the practice for themselves.

But not everyone. In every place I visited I found some who resisted what I was saying, and I thought it was important to try and understand them. Looking back on these experiences I can discern three kinds of objection: 1. it is too new, 2. it is too deep, and 3. it is not deep enough! The first was not so troubling. Those who found it 'too new' generally indicated that they were happy with the practice they already had, which was either the once-a-week meeting for worship or an alternative form of (daily) meditation. Some were too old, they admitted, to take on something so different from what they were used to. But whatever the reason, it was their choice not to try this 'new' approach for themselves.

The second objection was more serious. It was saying that it is not healthy to turn attention on yourself, to delve into the hidden depths of your own being. Who knows what you will find there? In any case, it is plainly selfish to think about yourself to the neglect of others. The true Quaker approach, some have said, is the opposite of that: to forget oneself and turn attention to other people. I could recognise a danger here, or rather their perception of danger, if the practice led to an exclusive preoccupation with oneself. But it has not been my experience that it does, or the experience of others who have adopted the practice. On the contrary, it tends to free people from self-preoccupation because it frees them from the anxiety that lies behind it. It is true, of course, that we do, to begin with, focus on ourselves, but we do this in the hope that in this way we can be rid of the feelings and illusions that make us insensitive to others. We can then, later, turn our attention to others more effectively. But with some Friends who have voiced this objection it is not so much a concern for others that touches them as an anxiety for themselves. What would they find if they looked directly at the reality of their lives, or unearthed the secrets of their hearts? Would they cope with this knowledge? Would they go crazy? Don't we need experts to help us in this area? I have to say that this objection has only been voiced by people who have not yet tried the practice, and usually as the reason for not trying it. Those who do try it soon come to realise that they are not in real danger in this meditative state of mind. The light that shows them the truth gives them at the same time the strength to accept it and the strength to deal with it in whatever way seems right. If they were relying on their normal human resources, it might indeed be frightening and even destabilising to look at the truth of one's life head on. But they are not. They are consciously letting all those faculties of reason and imagination go, so that they can see things in quite another way, objectively and 'coolly', which allows the divine source within them to come into play. Even so, it is natural to fear what one might find. And that, I sense, is the main obstacle to people trying it. I can only suggest that if people are anxious they should try the meditation on an issue that does not cause anxiety. They will then gain the confidence to try it again on something more serious. If some Friends are more than normally anxious, perhaps emotionally fragile or psychologically disturbed, they will need to be more cautious still. They may of course gain great insight from the practice, even some healing – I have known this to happen – but it might be risky if they were to practise initially on their own. They would do better to be with others who could support them, or specifically with a counsellor or therapist who was sympathetic to a meditative approach.[33] Gaining confidence and support in that way they would then be able to practise later on their own. But for most of us, whether fragile or relatively strong, the process of gaining trust and losing fear is a long and arduous one!

The third objection states that the practice is not deep enough. By focusing on the various 'issues of our lives', it claims, it fails to confront the really fundamental issue which is our pride and self-centredness. Only when we have let go of the self and surrendered to God are we in a position to experience the light that can illuminate our lives. This point is made by Friends who have experienced another form of spirituality where indeed self-surrender is the main demand, e.g. Indian advaita or Japanese zen.[34] When Friends say that they have tried the meditation, in a workshop for example, and that the experience was useful perhaps but not profound, I have to accept that. But if it leads them to take it no further that makes me sad. A forty minute meditation at a workshop can only be a beginning. If it shows any promise at all, it must be followed up with a regular practice. As you pursue the various issues that arise you will surely be led into deeper issues until eventually you reach the deepest issue of all, whatever that may be. You allow yourself to be led, at a pace that suits your own need, to the place where ultimately you want to go. That, as I understand it, is the Quaker way.

But these objections showed, even when misunderstandings were cleared, that the one-day workshop is not an ideal introduction for everyone. There are some people, though relatively few I have found, who need fuller explanation and discussion, or more time for the meditation itself, or the support of a small group of friends to follow it up. All this can be done by e.g. devoting a whole week to the process rather than one day, which we have tried on two occasions – I hope there will be more. It is also possible for Friends to form small groups to do the meditation regularly and support one another in it. But the discovery of this possibility has taken the work another step forward.

These 'light groups', as they have come to be called, were not initially an offshoot of the workshops. They began in late 1997 as a direct response to a talk I had given at Britain Yearly Meeting. A group of Friends from Norwich and Lynn Monthly Meeting decided that the only way to test the relevance of this practice of early Friends was to try it themselves! So, on the initiative of Alan Kirkham, they formed a number of small groups, between three and six in each, to 'wait together in the light' and share their experiences. Typically, the groups met for an hour and a half every two to three weeks in the home of a Friend. They insisted from the start that there should be regularity in attendance, therefore some commitment from each Friend from after the first meeting, and strict confidentiality within the group. All the groups would then gather for a meal in Norwich Meeting House every six weeks, to share their experience more widely and see what they could learn from one another. There are now, three years on, some ten groups still meeting at Norwich, and, through their influence, groups throughout the whole of their Monthly Meeting.

This development seemed so obviously right that I have been recommending the formation of light groups to anyone who showed interest, and so have many of the practitioners themselves, so that groups seem to be forming spontaneously.[35] In fact it seems to be necessary to the spirituality we are exploring. We have no masters, no gurus, no priests, yet we need other people to mirror back what is happening to us, and to make up for what is lacking in our individual experience and ability. Of course, this mutual need was the reason why Quakers met together from the beginning, but the modern Meeting doesn't often allow the kind of intimate sharing and self-exposure that is required. Friends need to get to know one another very well, building up the trust and confidence to enable them to speak with total honesty, and to listen with compassion. And this can happen much more easily in the small group where each person is committed to a search for truth, openness with others and strict confidentiality.[36] In this way, small light groups can be a great service to the larger Meeting, deepening the life of its members and preparing them 'in heart and mind' for their more public worship together.

But how do these discoveries affect the worship itself?

We have still to find an answer to this question. We have still to find ways of exploring the possibilities of public worship 'in spirit and in truth'. What difference would it make, for example, if we were to bring to the Meeting the honesty and openness we have discovered in private meditation and small group sharing? What would the worship itself be like if we could all transcend our individual interest and find unity in the truth? Could we also gain clarity about the world in the way we do about ourselves, from a discipline of waiting in the light?[37] But all this is a matter for further experiment, as more and more Friends become involved in the practice.

I want to conclude, though, by sharing my sense of gratitude, and awe, that so much has already been discovered. Those who have undertaken the exploration have found that the truth of their lives, which they may have been wary of before, is in fact liberating; that they have within them a capacity to see this truth and to embrace it which is quite different from their thinking and talking about it; that they can help one another to understand this reality and to live their lives on the basis of it, provided they share their experience honestly; and finally, that they can trust this light within them, this hidden divine source and power, whatever the situation they are in, whatever the difficulties they have to face. To me this is cause for wonder.

Appendix

Meditation Guides for
Workshops and Light Groups

The meditations are based on the practice of early Friends, as indicated, for example, in the epistles of George Fox and discussed in my paper 'The discipline of light', in my ed. *The Presence in the Midst* (Quaker Theology Seminar 1997). They have been given a present-day relevance and made usable in this workshop format with the help of Eugene Gendlin's book *Focusing* (Bantam Books, USA, 1981) in which he seems to have rediscovered (unknowingly) something of the original Quaker practice. Each of the six steps described here should last about six or seven minutes: the words of each paragraph should be read first, then followed by silence.

1. The individual

1. **Relax body and mind**. Start by making yourself perfectly comfortable. Feel the weight of your body on the chair (or the floor), then consciously release the tension in each part of your body. Then let all your immediate worries go, all your current preoccupations. Relax your mind so much that you give up 'talking to yourself' in your head. Let yourself become wholly receptive.

2. In this receptive state of mind, let **the real concerns of your life** emerge. Ask yourself, 'What is really going on in my life?', but do not try to answer the question. Let the answer come. You can be specific: 'What is happening in my relationships, my work, my Meeting, in my own heart and mind?' And more specifically still: 'Is there anything here that makes me feel uncomfortable, uneasy?' As we gradually become aware of these things we are beginning to experience the light.

3. Now **focus on one issue** that presents itself, one thing that gives you a sense of unease. And try to get a sense of this thing as a whole. Deep down you know what it is all about, but you don't normally allow yourself to take it all in and absorb the reality of it. Now is the time to do so. You don't have to get involved in this problem again, or get entangled with the feelings around it. Keep a little distance, so that you can see it clearly. Let the light show you what is really going on here. 'What is it about this thing', you can ask, 'that makes me feel uncomfortable?' Let the answer come. And when it does, let a word or image also come that says what it's really like, this thing that concerns me.

4. Now ask yourself **why it is like that**, or what makes it like that. Don't try to explain it. Just wait in the light till

you can see what it is. Let the answer come. If you get a simple answer like, 'Because I'm afraid' or 'Because that's the way she is', ask again the question why. 'Why am I afraid?', 'Why is she like that?' Let the full truth reveal itself, or as much truth as you are able to take at this moment. If you are really open and receptive, the answer will come.

5. When the answer comes **welcome it**. It may be painful, or difficult to believe with your normal conscious mind, but if it is the truth you will recognise it immediately and realise that it is something that you need to know. Trust the light. Say yes to it. Submit to it. It will then begin to heal you. It will show you new possibilities for your life. It will show you the way through. So however bad the news seems to be at first, accept it and let its truth pervade your whole being.

6. As soon as you accept what is being revealed to you, you will begin to **feel different**. Even bad news will seem strangely good. Accepting truth about yourself is like making peace. An inner conflict is being resolved. Now there is peace. Your body may respond quite noticeably to this change. A sense of relief may make you sigh, or want to laugh. Your diaphragm may heave. This is the beginning of changes that the light may bring about. But if none of this happens on this occasion do not worry. It may take longer. Notice how far you have got this time and pick it up on another occasion. In any case this is a process we do well to go through again and again, so that we can continue to grow and become more like the people we are meant to become.

When you feel ready, open your eyes, stretch your limbs, and bring the meditation to an end.

2. Other people

1. **Relax body and mind**. Start by making yourself perfectly comfortable. Notice how you are feeling in each part of your body, and consciously let go any tension or stiffness you feel there. Similarly with your mind: notice the thoughts and images that come to mind, then let them go. As much as possible, stop thinking altogether. Let yourself become wholly receptive.

2. In this receptive state of mind **let the people in your life emerge**, those who are close to you, those who are not so close. Consider the groups you are involved with, in your family, at work, in the neighbourhood or the city, among Quakers. Is there any group here, or any individual, who causes you some unease? Are you uncomfortable about your relationship, your involvement? What's the problem here? Don't answer yourself, with your own thoughts. Let the answer come. Let the light show you.

3. Now **focus on one group of people**, or, if you prefer, one individual, which gives you a sense of unease. Try to get a sense of these people (this person) as a whole. You know a lot about them already, but you naturally don't like to dwell on what makes you uncomfortable, or even to admit to yourself that things aren't quite right. But now you can. Now is the chance to recognise what's really going on. Ask yourself, again without answering, what is it about these people (this person) that disturbs me? Let the answer come in the silence. Let an image or word come that says what these people really mean to you, why they make you feel as you do.

4. Now ask yourself **what makes them like that**, why they are like that. Don't try to explain. Just wait, in the light, till you can see for yourself. If you lose your concentration, simply ask why? Keep asking why, then wait for an image, or a word, or a memory. Be open to surprises. Be open to the truth, and it will surely be revealed to you.

5. When the answer comes **welcome it**. This may not be easy at first, because it may not be something you want to hear or it may not be something you can readily believe. But if it is true you will know in your heart it is true, and you will know that you need to accept it. As soon as you do you will begin to feel different. You will feel a sense of release, of peace. A big issue in your life is being resolved.

6. Now finally, **consider how you need to act**. You won't need to weigh up 'pros' and 'cons' here, you will know in your heart what an appropriate response will be. What are you being called to do? How is the light leading you? It may be no different from what you have been doing for some time. It may be very different. Only you will know, as you open yourself to the truth. But recognising the truth, in the light, gives you a surprising certainty. Not about the whole answer, necessarily, but about the next step. And assuredly, when you take the next step you will understand the situation even better. And you will be able to act with confidence that you are being guided.

3. The Meeting

1. **Relax body and mind**. Start by making yourself perfectly comfortable. Feel the weight of your body on the chair, then consciously release the tension in each part of your body. Try to let all your immediate worries go, all your current preoccupations. Relax your mind as much as possible, so that you give up 'talking to yourself' in your head, but remain alert and aware. Let yourself become wholly receptive.

2. In this receptive state of mind, let **the real concerns of your Meeting** emerge. Ask yourself, 'What is really going on in my Meeting?', but do not try to answer the question. Let the answer come. You can be quite specific: 'What is happening in our relationships, our worship, our work together, and my involvement with the whole group?' And more specifically still: 'Is there anything here that makes me feel uncomfortable, uneasy?' As we gradually become aware of these things we are beginning to see one another in the light.

3. Now **focus on one issue** that presents itself, one thing that gives you a sense of unease. And try to get a sense of this thing as a whole. Deep down you know what it is all about, but you don't normally allow yourself to take it all in and absorb the reality of it. Now is the time to do so. You don't have to get involved in this problem again, or get entangled with the feelings around it. Keep a little distance, so that you can see it more clearly. Let the light show you what is really going on here. 'What is it about this thing', you can ask, 'that makes me feel uncomfortable?' Let the answer come. And when it does, let a word or image also come that says what it's really like, this thing that concerns me.

4. Now ask yourself **why it is like that**, or what makes it like that. Don't try to explain it. Just wait, in the light, till you can see for yourself. If you get a simple answer like, 'Because they're afraid' or 'Because that's the way he is', ask again the question why. 'Why are they afraid?', 'Why is he like that?' Let the full truth reveal itself, or as much truth as you are able to take at this moment. If you are really open and receptive, the answer will come.

5. When the answer comes **welcome it**. It may be painful, or difficult to believe with your normal conscious mind, but if it is the truth you will recognise it immediately, and know that it is something that you need to know. Trust the light. Say yes to it. Submit to it. It will then begin to heal you, and your Meeting. It will show you new possibilities for your life together. It will show you the way through. So however bad the news seems to be at first, accept it and let its truth pervade your whole being.

6. Now finally, **consider how you need to act**. You won't need to weigh up pros and cons here, you will know in your heart what an appropriate response will be. So ask: 'What am I being called to do here?' It may in fact be no different from what you have been doing for some time. But it may be very different. Only you will know, as you open yourself to the truth. But recognising the truth, in the light, gives you a surprising certainty. Not about the whole answer, necessarily, but about the next step. And assuredly, when you take the next step you will understand the situation even better. And you will be able to act with confidence that you are being guided.

When you feel ready, open your eyes, stretch your limbs, and bring the meditation to an end.

4. The group

This is a variation on meditation 3, for 'the Meeting', but now the focus of attention is on a group that has come together for a very particular purpose. The process spelled out in the previous meditations will be taken for granted in this one, so the questions will be brief. They can also be changed to suit the nature of the group, perhaps in conjunction with the group itself, which can then design its own meditation. The suggested model here was devised for a support group for refugees.

1. What is the group for?
2. How can we best achieve this?
3. How can we best work together?
4. What are my own strengths in relation to this group?
5. What are my weaknesses in relation to this group?
6. What is my place in the group?

5. The world

1. **Relax body and mind**. Start by making yourself perfectly comfortable. Feel the weight of your body on the chair, then consciously release the tension in each part of your body. Now let all your immediate worries go; in particular, let go of any images or stories of the world that have touched you recently from television and newspapers. We want to know the truth about our world. So let yourself become wholly receptive.

2. In this receptive state of mind, let **the real issues of the world** emerge. Ask yourself: 'What is really going on in the world? What is happening in the world as I know it, as I experience it?' And be specific: '...in the world of work, of commerce, politics'. Is there anything there that makes you feel uncomfortable? Don't try to answer

yourself. Let the answer come. Let the light show you what is happening.

3. **Now focus on one issue** that presents itself, one thing that gives you a sense of unease. Try to get a sense of this thing as a whole. And ask yourself: 'What is it about this situation, those events, those people that makes me feel uncomfortable?' Let the truth disclose itself. And when it does, let a word or image come that says what it's really like, what it is that touches you.

4. Now ask yourself **what makes it like that**. Don't try to explain. Just wait in the light till you can see for yourself. If you lose your concentration, simply ask why? Keep asking why, then wait for an image, a word, a memory. Be open to the truth, hard though it may be, and it will surely be revealed to you.

5. When the answer comes, **welcome it**. It may be surprising, even difficult to believe. It may not fit in with what you want to believe, or what you have seen and heard by others. But if it fits your own experience you will know immediately that it is true. And accepting that it's true will bring a sense of peace, and a freedom from the worry that has surrounded this issue.

6. Now finally, **consider how you need to act**. You won't need to weigh up alternatives or think through strategies. You will know in your heart what an appropriate response will be. What are you being called to do? How is the light leading you? Is it to do what you have already been doing for some time? Or is it to do something different? Only you will know, as you open yourself to the truth.

When you are ready, open your eyes, stretch your limbs, and bring the meditation to an end.

NOTES

1   The dissertation was later written up as a book and published: Rosemary Moore, *The Light in their Consciences: the early Quakers in Britain 1646-1666*, Penn State University Press, 2000.

2   Published by William Eerdmans, Grand Rapids, Michigan, 1973.

3   Hugh Barbour and Arthur O. Roberts, eds., *Early Quaker Writings 1650-1700*, Eerdmans, Grand Rapids, Michigan, 1973, pp. 22f.

4   Margaret Fell, *Works of Margaret Fell*, pp. 95, 136; quoted in Hugh Barbour, *The Quakers in Puritan England*, Yale University Press, 1964, p. 98.

5   *The Quakers in Puritan England*, pp. 98f, 102f.

6   *The Quakers in Puritan England*, pp. 108f.

7   Published in 1831, reprinted in 1990 as a New Foundation Publication by the George Fox Fund, State College, Pennsylvania. The first two of the eight volumes are the Ellwood edition of the Journal, with the many letters and papers of Fox which Ellwood had inserted there.

8   George Fox, *To all that would know the way to the kingdom*, 1653, in *Works* 4:17. Cf. the earlier version, ed. Joseph Pickvance, *To all that would know the way to the kingdom*, The George Fox Project Trust, 2001, pp. 4f. For the quotation from Pickvance see his Introduction, p. i.

9 One outcome of this study was a compilation of the clearest and most profound writing of Fox, which was later published with a glossary, interpretive essay, and translation into modern English: Rex Ambler, *Truth of the Heart: an anthology of George Fox 1624-91*, Quaker Books, London, 2001 – referred to in these notes as *TOTH*. I am at present working on an anthology of the other Quaker writers of the period, with the probable title *Experiment upon the Soul*, to be published, I hope, in 2002.

10 From the American diary, 1672, in *Journal*, ed. J. Nickalls, Oxford University Press, 1952, p. 639; *TOTH*, 1:44.

11 George Fox, *Journal*, ed. J. Nickalls, Oxford University Press, 1952, p. 400; *TOTH*, 3:42.

12 George Fox, Epistle 10 (1652), *Works* 7:20; *TOTH*, 1:90.

13 I made a similar attempt some years ago, in 1996, and drew up a nine-step process, which I called, somewhat tongue-in-cheek, Fox's 'experiment with light'. But I was describing then the larger process of waiting in the light *and* living by it. The titles were my own, they were these: 1. turn inside, 2. identify the light, 3. let the light show you yourself, 4. trace the light to its source, 5. trust the light to show you the alternatives, 6. feel the new life grow, 7. see others in the light, 8. see the world in the light, and 9. learn to love in the light. Here 1 and 2 correspond to step 1 in my new scheme, 3 corresponds to 2, 4 and 5 to 3. 'Submitting' was included in the description but not as a separate step. That brief statement was in fact a summary of a much longer paper, 'The discipline of light', presented to the Quaker Theology Seminar early that year, as my first attempt to articulate this new understanding. See note 31, below.

14 A paper of 1654, *Doctrinals*, *Works* 4:43; *TOTH*, 1:83.

15 A paper of 1656 added to Fox's *Journal* by the first editor, Thomas Ellwood, *Works* 1:295; *TOTH*, 1:82.

16 George Fox, Epistle 34 (1653), *Works* 7:42; *TOTH*, 1:68.

17 George Fox, Epistle 149 (1657), *Works* 7:142; *TOTH*, 1:81.

18 Epistle 11 (1652), *Works* 7:21; *TOTH*, 1:86.

19 See p. 9 above and note 8.

20 George Fox, *Journal*, ed. J. Nickalls, letter to Lady Claypool, pp. 346-8; *TOTH* 1:61, 91. Fox comments in his *Journal*, after quoting the letter in full, 'she said it settled and stayed her mind for the present. And many Friends got copies of it, both in England and Ireland, to read it to distracted people; and it settled several of their minds.'

21 George Fox, Epistle 10 (1652), *Works* 7:20; *TOTH*, 1:90.

22 Thomas Ellwood, *The History of the Life of Thomas Ellwood*, quoted in Jessamyn West, ed., *The Quaker Reader*, Pendle Hill Publications, Wallingford, Pennsylvania, 1992, p. 149.

23 On the pattern of early Quaker experience see Howard Brinton, *Quaker Journals: varieties of religious experience among Friends*, Pendle Hill 1972, as well as the works of Hugh Barbour already referred to, especially 'The Power and Terror of the Light', in *Quakers in Puritan England*, pp. 94-126.

24 Eugene Gendlin, *Focusing*, Bantam Books, revised ed. 1981 and subsequently, pp. 3f.

25 Op. cit., p. 4.

26 Op. cit., p. 9.

27 Op. cit., pp. 43-5.

28 Ann Weiser Cornell, *The Power of Focusing*, New Harbinger Publications, Oakland, California, 1996, p. 3.

29 Op. cit., p. viii; cf. p. 70 where she distinguishes the 'voice of truth' inside from 'your inner critic'.

30 We cannot infer from this that no one found difficulty with what was recommended. It is quite possible that many did, but had no reason to write down their experience. However, I have come across two examples of people who struggled with the process, though they seem to have been aware of what they should be doing. One is Princess Elizabeth of the Rhine, who was eager to discover for herself the spirituality that Quakers from Britain were talking about. She had been visited in Germany by Robert Barclay, a cousin of hers, and by other leading Friends. But she wrote to him as follows: 'Now that I have sometimes a small glimpse of the true light, I do not attend to it as I should, being drawn away by the works of my calling which must be done.' (Letter of 24 June 1676, in Maria Webb, *The Fells of Swarthmoor Hall*, Philadelphia, 1896, pp. 327f.) Another friend of Barclay, Anna Maria, Countess of Horne, wrote to him in a similar vein: 'It may at times thus fare with me, that the inward witness testifies and calleth to me in my soul, and I, because I know not his voice nor the testimony thereof, do pass it by, looking upon it as the voice of a stranger. For want of this spirit of discerning, I come many times to behave myself as an enemy in not receiving his testimony....I know he calls me: O that I did but always know his voice, and know what he requires of me. Now my place appears to be in silence, to be still, and wait upon the Lord there.' (Op. cit., p. 329.)

31 The very first attempt was only a week before: I gave an academic paper to the Quaker Theology Seminar on the significance of 'light'. It was published in the Proceedings of that year, *The Presence in the Midst*, by QTS and Woodbrooke, 1997.

32 Published by the Hanover Group of the Religious Society of Friends in Germany, Bad Pyrmont, in 1996.

The talk itself was published later that year in *Der Quäker*, July 1996, and a year after that in an English version: 'Quaker identity: anything goes?', *The Friends Quarterly*, October 1997. *Wo Worte enden* was the German edition of a book previously published in English as *The End of Words: issues in contemporary Quaker theology*, Quaker Home Service, 1994.

33 Some psychotherapists now use focusing as part of their practice: cf. Eugene Gendlin's own work on this, *Focusing-Oriented Psychotherapy: a manual of the experiential method*, Guildford Press, New York and London, 1996. Others use meditative practices derived from Buddhism: cf. John Welwood, ed., *Awakening the Heart: east/west approaches to psychotherapy and the healing relationship*, Shambhala, Boston and London, 1983; Mark Epstein, *Thoughts without a Thinker: psychotherapy from a Buddhist perspective*, Duckworth, London, 1996.

34 I don't as yet have a full answer to this point of comparison, partly because I need to know more about the spiritualities concerned before I can compare them. There can be no doubt that spiritualities differ in their emphasis, and that what is central for one is not quite central for another. But each has its own 'way', and that way has to be followed to gain the enlightenment promised. Some rely on the liturgies and disciplines of the church, e.g. the Christian mystics of the middle-ages, some rely on physical and mental exercises, e.g. yoga and tai chi. But what, I ask, is the distinctive Quaker way? We have rejected most of the religious disciplines that have been available to us and turned consciously to 'the light within'. But this is not to say, and it was never said, that if we turn inside we will immediately experience God. We, too, have to follow a way, but it is a way that begins with ourselves in the condition we are in. It begins in our 'conscience', our awareness of things that are not quite right, and it leads from there to an awareness of ourselves, and from there to an awareness of other people and of God, provided that at each step we accept the truth being shown to us. We might say that the Quaker way begins in the shallows, with our everyday awareness, but then leads us little by little into the depths where we no longer have words to describe what we see.

35 In fact, groups that are working well tend to spread the word in their Meeting, or more widely still. There are a couple of groups that travel in their Monthly Meeting to introduce other Friends to the practice and to help them establish a group of their own. Some Friends run workshops themselves or retreats where they teach the practice, though *how* it is taught differs widely. There is also a set of tapes that introduce the practice: one explains the process as it was developed by early Friends, the other takes people through the meditation so that they can try it for themselves. In fact many groups continue to use the tape, or make one of their own, because that frees everyone to participate. After a while though, as Friends become confident in the process, they can dispense with a guide altogether. There is great variety in the ways groups meet together – some going for walks, some communicating by the internet – but there seems to be a standard pattern in the way they spend their time. They socialise to begin with, catching up on one another, perhaps share a meal, then do the meditation together, with or without a tape. Afterwards they have time by themselves, individually, to make notes or pictures or otherwise absorb what occurred in the meditation. They will then listen to each other as they share what they can or wish to of what happened, but without discussion or advice. When all have been heard they can then conclude with discussion and chat about the things that arose. I don't think anyone has counted the number of groups that now exist, but my guess would be that there are between fifty and sixty, including those in continental Europe and North America. It would be helpful if someone could make a study of this phenomenon. What information we have is available from the contact person of 'experiment with light', Charlie Blackfield; www.charlieblackfield.com/light/index.htm

36 This was the case at the beginning: remember the description of those early meetings in the first quotations from Barbour and Roberts. 'In the little groups of Meetings those who had gone through the experience could help those still wrestling with the deeper discoveries of self-deception.' Compare the account in the book Barbour later wrote with William Frost, *The Quakers* (Friends United Press, Richmond, Indiana, 1988, p. 39): 'Hearers who were "convinced" by these forms of mission were taken into smaller gatherings in private homes, where they shared their struggles of self-judgment under the Light with other seekers in daily or weekly "gathered meetings" with prayer and messages of guidance as well as silence and tears.'

37 I have sometimes used a meditation guide for this purpose in workshops and training sessions. A copy is attached in the Appendix: '5. the world'.